SEP 0 7 2004

LAURA INGALLS WILDER

DISCOVER THE LIFE OF AN AMERICAN LEGEND

David and Patricia Armentrout

Rourke
Publishing LLC
Vero Beach, Florida 32964

www.rourkepublishing.com

PHOTO CREDITS: © PhotoDisc Title page, page 8; "Laura Ingalls Wilder Home and Museum, Mansfield, Missouri" all other photos

Cover: *Laura Ingalls Wilder around the age of 39*

Title page : *Pioneer families in the late 1800s traveled by covered wagon.*

Editor: Frank Sloan

Cover design by Nicola Stratford

Library of Congress Cataloging-in-Publication Data

Armentrout, David, 1962-
Laura Ingalls Wilder / David and Patricia Armentrout.
   v. cm. -- (Discover the life of an American legend)
Includes bibliographical references and index.
Contents: Pioneer girl — Laura's family — Life on the prairie —
Pioneer hardships — Almanzo Wilder — A time for change — Rocky Ridge Farm — Laura's new career —
Little House books — Dates to remember.
   ISBN 1-58952-663-5 (hardcover)
1. Wilder, Laura Ingalls, 1867-1957—Juvenile literature. 2. Authors, American—20th century—Biography—
Juvenile literature. 3. Women pioneers—United States—Biography—Juvenile literature. 4. Frontier and
pioneer life—United States—Juvenile literature. 5. Children's stories—Authorship—Juvenile literature. [1.
Wilder, Laura Ingalls, 1867-1957. 2. Authors, American. 3. Women—Biography.] I. Armentrout, Patricia,
1960- II. Title. III. Series.
PS3545.I342Z568 2003
813'.52—dc21
                                                    2003002208

Printed in the USA

CG/CG

Table of Contents

Pioneer Girl   5

Laura's Family   6

Life on the Prairie   9

Pioneer Hardships   11

Almanzo Wilder   13

A Time for Change   14

Rocky Ridge Farm   16

Laura's New Career   19

Little House Books   20

Dates to Remember   22

Glossary   23

Index   24

Further Reading/Websites to Visit   24

Pioneer Girl

Laura Ingalls was born in Wisconsin in 1867. Her parents were Charles and Caroline. Laura called them Ma and Pa.

Laura moved many times during her childhood. Her father was a **pioneer** and was always in search of a better way of life. When Laura grew up, she wrote about life as a pioneer girl. Her writings became the famous "Little House" books.

Laura Ingalls Wilder painted a picture of pioneer life with her "Little House" Books.

Laura's Family

Laura lived in Indian Territory in Kansas, in Walnut Grove, Minnesota, and in Burr Oak, Iowa. In 1879 her family moved to De Smet in Dakota Territory.

Laura had three sisters. Mary was the oldest. Then came Laura, Carrie, and Grace. Mary became blind at the age of 14. Laura decided she would become Mary's eyes. Laura enjoyed describing everything to Mary.

Life on the Prairie

Laura's chores included bringing in the cows from the pasture and helping in the kitchen. When weather permitted, Laura and her sisters walked to school.

Laura also managed to have fun. She loved running barefoot through the tall grass and letting the wind blow through her hair. Laura loved being outdoors on the **prairie**.

Laura loved to explore the open prairie.

Pioneer Hardships

The Ingalls family went through **hardships**, like many other pioneer families. For example, in Walnut Grove grasshoppers ruined the wheat crop two years in a row. Laura's Pa had to walk 200 miles (320 kilometers) to look for work. In De Smet, the winter blizzards of 1880-81 nearly caused starvation. The railroad was shut down because of the snow. Food and coal delivery did not begin again until spring.

Carrie and Laura with Ma and Pa Ingalls

Almanzo Wilder

In 1883, Laura accepted a teaching job 12 miles (19.3 km) from De Smet. Almanzo Wilder, a family friend, took Laura to and from her job every weekend. Soon Laura and Almanzo began a **courtship**. In August of 1885 Laura and Almanzo married. The next year their daughter Rose was born.

Laura and Almanzo posed for this portrait shortly after their marriage.

A Time for Change

The Wilders suffered crop failure, hail, fire, and illness during their first few years of marriage. Laura also had a son who died 12 days after he was born.

In 1894, Laura, Almanzo, and Rose traveled by covered wagon for 45 days and finally settled in Mansfield, Missouri. Laura was delighted to see lush green woods instead of dry prairie grasses.

Rose Wilder around age three

Rocky Ridge Farm

The Wilders bought 40 acres (16 hectares) and called their land Rocky Ridge Farm. Over the years Laura and Almanzo raised chickens and horses and grew apple trees.

Rose became a writer when she grew up. She traveled all over the world. Laura and Almanzo became successful poultry farmers.

Rocky Ridge Farm, where Laura developed her writing talents

Laura's New Career

At age 44, Laura began a new career. She wrote newspaper articles about farm life. Laura also wrote down her childhood memories. Rose helped Laura with her writing.

In 1932, at the age of 65, Laura's first book, *Little House in the Big Woods*, was published. It was a great success. Children all over the country loved Laura's book about pioneer life.

Laura and Almanzo in their later years at Rocky Ridge

Little House Books

Laura was 76 when she finished her eighth "Little House" book. Her books are now classics and known worldwide.

Laura and Almanzo lived long, hard, but fulfilling lives. Almanzo died in 1949 at the age of 92. Laura was 90 when she died in 1957.

Today, Rocky Ridge Farm is the Laura Ingalls Wilder Home and Museum. Many people visit the site to honor and remember Laura.

Young readers surround Laura at a book signing in 1952.

Dates to Remember

1867	Born February 7 in Pepin County, Wisconsin
1875	Grasshoppers destroy crops in Minnesota
1880	The Ingalls family suffers through winter blizzards
1883	Laura begins teaching
1885	Laura and Almanzo Wilder marry August 25
1886	Rose is born December 5
1894	Laura, Almanzo, and Rose move to Mansfield, Missouri
1932	First "Little House" book is published
1949	Almanzo dies
1957	Laura dies

Glossary

courtship (KORT ship) — attempts by one person to win the love and affection of another.

hardships (HARD ships) — things that cause difficulty or suffering

pioneer (pye uh NEER) — someone who moves to and settles unknown territory

prairie (PRAYR ee) — a large area of flat or rolling grassland with few or no trees

Index

Burr Oak, Iowa   6
De Smet, Dakota Territory   6,
    11, 13
Ingalls, Caroline   5
Ingalls, Charles   5, 11
"Little House" books   5, 19, 20

Mansfield, Missouri   14
Rocky Ridge Farm   16, 20
Walnut Grove, Minnesota   6,
    11
Wilder, Almanzo   13, 14, 16,
    20
Wilder, Rose   13, 14, 16, 19

Further Reading

Anderson, William. *Pioneer Girl: The Story of Laura Ingalls Wilder*. Harper Trophy, 2000.
Wadsworth, Ginger. *Laura Ingalls Wilder*. Lerner, 1997.

Websites To Visit

www.lauraingallswilderhome.com
www.littlehousebooks.com
www.liwms.com/

About The Authors

David and Patricia Armentrout have written many nonfiction books for young readers. They specialize in science and social studies topics. They have had several books published for primary school reading. The Armentrouts live in Cincinnati, Ohio, with their two children.